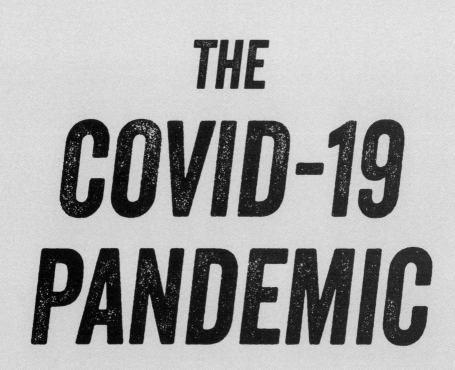

THE COVID-19 PANDEMIC

THE COVID-19 PANDEMIC

A Coronavirus Timeline

MATT DOEDEN

LERNER PUBLICATIONS ◆ MINNEAPOLIS

Lerner Publications Company
An imprint of Lerner Publishing Group, Inc.
241 First Avenue North
Minneapolis, MN 55401 USA

For reading levels and more information, look up this title at www.lernerbooks.com.

Image credits: Centers for Disease Control and Prevention Public Health Image Library, pp. 2, 3, 4; Novac Vitali/Shutterstock.com, p. 8; sleepingpanda/Shutterstock.com, p. 9; Binturong-tonoscarpe/ Shutterstock.com, p. 10; Cristina Stoian/Shutterstock.com, p. 11; AP Photo/FeatureChina, p. 12; AP Photo/Hong Hae-in/Yonhap, p. 13; AP Photo/Chinatopix, p. 14; AP Photo/Yomiuri Shimbun, p. 17; AP Photo/Elaine Thompson, p. 19; AP Photo/Rich Pedroncelli, p. 21; AP Photo/VWPics, p. 22; AP Photo/Fabian Sommer/picture-alliance/dpa, p. 23; Lisa Trowse/EyeEm/Getty Images, p. 24; Álvaro Calvo/Getty Images, p. 26; Laura Westlund/Independent Picture Service, pp. 27, 35; AP Photo/ Nicole Hester/MLive.com/Ann Arbor News, p. 28; AP Photo/Andrew Harnik, p. 29; Grace Cary/ Getty Images, p. 31; AP Photo/Ron Adar/SOPA Images/Sipa USA, p. 33 (top); Stephen Maturen/ Getty Images, p. 33 (bottom); AP Photo/Alex Brandon, p. 37; AP Photo/Braulio Jatar/SOPA Images, p. 38; ER Productions Limited/DigitalVision/Getty Images, p. 39.

Cover: Karen Ducey/Getty Images; Centers for Disease Control and Prevention Public HealthImage Library; Noam Galai/Getty Images.

Main body text set in Rotis Serif Std 55.
Typeface provided by Adobe Systems.

Editor: Alison Lorenz

Library of Congress Cataloging-in-Publication Data

Names: Doeden, Matt, author.
Title: The COVID-19 pandemic : a coronavirus timeline / Matt Doeden.
Description: Minneapolis : Lerner Publications, 2021 | Series: Gateway biographies | Includes bibliographical references and index. | Audience: Ages 9–14 | Audience: Grades 4–6 | Summary: "In 2019 a new, deadly coronavirus appeared and quickly spread around the world. This issue biography follows the timeline of the COVID-19 pandemic, examines its impact on society, explains the US government's response, and more"– Provided by publisher.
Identifiers: LCCN 2020028325 (print) | LCCN 2020028326 (ebook) | ISBN 9781728427706 (library binding) | ISBN 9781728427713 (ebook)
Subjects: LCSH: COVID-19 (Disease)–United States–Juvenile literature. | Epidemics–United States– Juvenile literature. | COVID-19 (Disease)–Social aspects–United States–Juvenile literature. | COVID-19 (Disease)–Government policy–United States–Juvenile literature.
Classification: LCC RA644.C67 D64 2021 (print) | LCC RA644.C67 (ebook) | DDC 614.5/924140973–dc23

LC record available at https://lccn.loc.gov/2020028325
LC ebook record available at https://lccn.loc.gov/2020028326

Manufactured in the United States of America
3-52457-49448-2/28/2022

TABLE OF CONTENTS

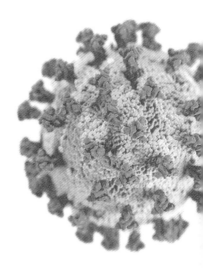

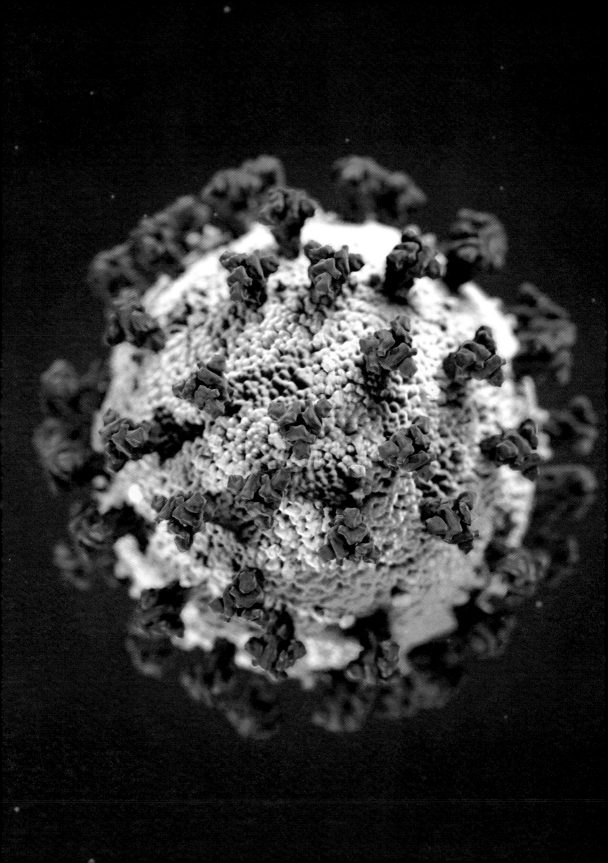

When fifty-two-year-old Michael Kevin Rathel got sick in late March 2020, he got really sick. Rathel and his family contracted a virus that was new to human beings. The disease it caused, called COVID-19, hit him hard. While Rathel's family suffered only mild symptoms, Rathel's symptoms were anything but.

By April 2, Rathel could barely walk. He struggled for breath. His wife, Stacie, rushed him to the nearest hospital in Orlando, Florida. There his condition worsened. Doctors put him in a coma, a common practice for patients in extreme distress.

Rathel faced a grim outlook. Doctors didn't know how to treat the new disease. They put Rathel on a ventilator to help him breathe. But he didn't improve.

Stacie searched desperately for any bit of information that could help. She read that blood plasma from people who had survived COVID-19 might help those in severe distress. She was still recovering, so she couldn't donate. A family friend took up the search for a donor.

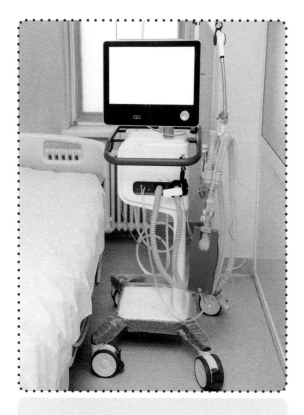

A ventilator is a machine doctors use to help patients breathe.

He found James Crocker. Crocker had recently recovered from COVID-19, and his blood type matched Rathel's. Crocker donated blood, and on April 8, doctors transfused the plasma into Rathel's body. Then they waited.

Rathel slowly improved. On April 12, doctors brought him out of his coma. He was groggy and confused. He spoke to his family over video chat. "You're alive, and you're going to make it," his wife told him. On April 16, doctors took him off the ventilator. For the first time in more than a week, he was breathing on his own. Rathel was on his way to a long recovery.

No one can say for sure what brought Rathel back from the brink of death. But his family believes that a gift from a stranger saved his life.

Not everyone was so lucky. The virus that caused COVID-19 was spreading like wildfire. It was infecting people by the thousands. The mysterious disease was about to change the world forever.

The city of Wuhan in Hubei Province, China

MAKING THE JUMP

In late 2019, medical professionals became aware of a new illness rapidly spreading through the Chinese city of Wuhan. Dozens of patients showed signs of pneumonia, an infection that inflames the lungs, and other symptoms. Doctors scrambled to find the cause. Within days they identified a virus that was new to humans. Over the following months, scientists pieced together the origin of the virus, later named SARS-CoV-2. Often, viruses cannot spread from one type of mammal to another. Most viruses adapt to infect just one type of host. But some make the leap to humans. After much research, Chinese scientists came to believe SARS-CoV-2 started in bats.

The virus was probably present in bats for a long time. At some point, it mutated, or its genetic code changed. The change meant the virus was able to infect new hosts. Scientists don't know for sure how many different animal species it could infect. But they are sure it infected pangolins.

Bats carry many viruses, though most of them do not infect humans.

Pangolins are small, scaly mammals that are native to Asia and Africa. When the virus infected them, it borrowed some of their genetic code. The virus may have continued to jump among animals after pangolins. But the bit of pangolins' genetic code was the key that allowed it to infect human beings.

When and how humans first caught the virus is a mystery. One theory argues it may have happened at a wet market, a place where live animals are sold. Another theory claims that the virus first infected dogs, who then passed it to their owners. No matter where it first appeared, once the virus infected humans, it spread quickly. Some people who caught it became very ill. Others showed mild symptoms or no symptoms.

A market in Chinatown in Yangon, Myanmar

Those with mild infections went about their business, unknowingly spreading the virus to many others.

China and other nations tried to contain the virus. But SARS-CoV-2 was circulating widely before anyone realized it.

EARLY RESPONSE

In December 2019, Chinese ophthalmologist Dr. Li Wenliang noticed something troubling in some of his patients. They were suffering from an illness that seemed familiar to him. Its symptoms looked a lot like severe acute respiratory

After his death, Li was memorialized for his early warnings about a possible outbreak.

syndrome, or SARS. SARS, identified in 2003, was highly deadly. An outbreak of the disease that year had been one of the most fearsome viral outbreaks in decades.

Li was worried. On December 30, he posted a message online to warn fellow doctors to protect themselves from a possible new outbreak. But when Wuhan's Public Security Bureau found out about the message, they reprimanded Li and forced him to sign a letter saying that his claims were false. In truth, Li had not been the only one to notice the outbreak. China's government was eager to control news on the new threat.

Li continued to treat patients. Then, on January 10, he developed a cough. A fever soon followed. Within three days, he was in the hospital, battling the same symptoms he had noticed in his patients. Li was diagnosed with the new coronavirus on January 30. On February 7, he died from complications of the disease.

Meanwhile, the world slowly became aware of the threat that had alarmed Li. Officials in Wuhan first spoke publicly about the new disease on December 31, 2019. They knew it wasn't SARS, but it was similar. Like SARS and the closely related MERS (Middle East respiratory syndrome), the disease was caused by a type of virus called a coronavirus. It was unclear how the new virus spread, but it seemed to settle in the lungs of those it infected. Doctors scrambled to treat patients who were struggling to breathe. For the most severe cases, they had no answers. China reported its first death on January 11.

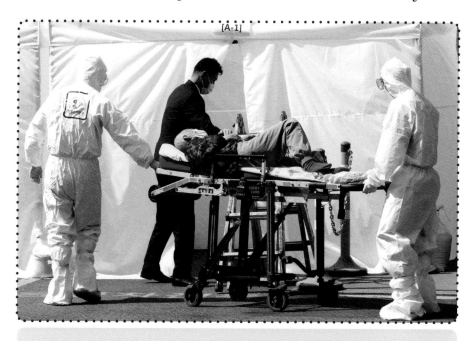

Workers transport a patient suspected to have MERS in South Korea in 2015.

Dr. Zhong Nanshan, who helped China through the SARS outbreak in 2003, began to lead a team to investigate the new coronavirus. Zhong traveled to Wuhan on January 18 and spoke to local officials. They soon confirmed that the virus could spread from person to person. China began to lock down Wuhan a few days later. Nations around the world began fully or partially closing their borders to travelers from China, including the United States on January 31. The bans may have

An officer takes a driver's temperature at a highway checkpoint in Wuhan, China.

helped to slow the spread of the disease. But they came too late to stop it.

By the time the first travel bans were issued, the virus had already moved outside of China. Thailand reported its first case on January 13. Japan, South Korea, Taiwan, and Hong Kong soon followed. On January 21, the United States reported its first case, a man in Washington State who had visited Wuhan. Soon the United States identified its first case of community spread. This meant the new patient had not been to China but had contracted the virus from someone in the community.

Many experts focused on trying to contain the disease. But hopes of stopping its spread were fading. The reported cases were often only the most severe, meaning far more infections were going undiscovered. Most people who caught the virus showed only mild or no symptoms. Many never even knew they had it—but they still could spread it. Through these quiet transmissions, the virus spread more and more each day.

Throughout February and early March, Wuhan remained the center of the outbreak in the eyes of the world. The city's hospitals were filled with people struggling to breathe, and the Chinese government rushed to build new hospitals to treat the overflow of patients. Hotels became sites to quarantine people who had been exposed. The United States and other nations hurried to evacuate citizens who had traveled to Wuhan and couldn't get back home. As the death toll grew, many experts warned that a global pandemic was looming.

GOING GLOBAL

On January 20, the *Diamond Princess*, a luxury cruise ship, set sail from Japan carrying 2,666 passengers and 1,045 crew. Among them was an eighty-year-old Chinese man who developed a cough as the ship began its voyage. He may have been carrying the SARS-CoV-2 virus. Or the virus may have come aboard with someone else. But once on the tightly packed ship, it spread like wildfire.

People started to get sick. Many of the ship's passengers were older, and the virus tended to hit people over the age of sixty-five the hardest. To try to stop the virus's spread, the ship went under quarantine. People had to stay in their rooms, many of which were tiny interior cabins. The staff was forced to keep working despite the high risk of infection. "Anybody would be scared for their life, because day by day more and more people were getting infected," said one crew member. "And we knew people were dying."

By February 7, sixty-one people aboard the ship had tested positive for the disease. The *Diamond Princess* searched for a place to let its passengers off. But no country wanted to take the risk. Instead, nations began working to rescue their citizens. On February 16, the United States evacuated more than three hundred US citizens from the ship, flew them back to the US, and placed them under quarantine. By March 1, all the *Diamond Princess*'s passengers had left the ship. More than seven hundred people had contracted the virus while aboard, and six died from it. The story played out again

and again as other cruise ships suffered outbreaks and were forced to quarantine passengers.

It was a sign of how quickly the virus was going global. New hot spots erupted in other countries such as Italy and Iran. By early March, Italy's hospitals were overrun with patients of the new disease, now called COVID-19 (short for coronavirus disease 2019, the year the disease emerged). Italy struggled to provide enough doctors, hospital beds, and medical gear such as personal protective equipment (PPE) and ventilators.

Experts in the United States grew more and more uneasy. They still didn't know much about the virus. Because few countries were able to test people for the virus on a large scale, it was impossible to know the death rates from COVID-19. The disease was especially dangerous for older adults and for those who had existing medical conditions such as lung cancer. And though most who caught it seemed to have mild symptoms, the long-term effects of the disease on even young, healthy people were unclear. Researchers kept working to find more answers.

After the few initial cases were reported, the virus kept spreading in the US. Messages about the disease and its severity were mixed. Many experts gave dire warnings. But some politicians, including President Donald Trump, downplayed the dangers. "This is going to go away without a vaccine, it's [going to] go away, and we're not going to see it again, hopefully, after a period of time," Trump told reporters.

Washington State experienced the first US outbreak. The state announced its first death on February 29, 2020. It later reported that two other deaths on February 26 were from COVID-19. Many of Washington's cases were tied to long-term care facilities. Staff at such facilities around the country asked how they could protect the vulnerable adults in their care.

Meanwhile, the threat of a COVID-19 outbreak began to change how people behaved. Experts encouraged people to practice physical distancing—also called social distancing—by staying at least 6 feet (2 m) apart from those outside their households. Some took the recommendation to heart. But others ignored it. They did not believe the virus posed a great threat.

Staff members load a patient into an ambulance in Kirkland, Washington.

LOCKDOWN

On March 11, the Utah Jazz and the Oklahoma City Thunder of the National Basketball Association (NBA) were preparing to play a regular-season game. Earlier that day, the World Health Organization had labeled COVID-19 a pandemic—a worldwide crisis. Yet the arena in Oklahoma City was packed with fans. Players, coaches, and officials were on the court. Tip-off was just minutes away.

Then a team doctor rushed onto the court to talk with the officials. He told them that a member of the Jazz,

Rudy Gobert, had tested positive for COVID-19. The game was delayed as the NBA league office decided what to do.

The league postponed the game. An hour later, the NBA announced that it would put the season on hold. Other sports leagues quickly followed, including the National Hockey League. That evening Trump announced an order banning foreign nationals from most European countries from entering the US. For many Americans, the day marked a new stage of the outbreak. COVID-19 was changing fundamental parts of life across the nation. Clearly, business as usual was no longer an option.

Federal, state, and local leaders faced difficult decisions. COVID-19 was spreading rapidly. It threatened to overwhelm hospitals with more patients than they could handle. On March 13, Trump declared the virus a national emergency. A few days later, California governor Gavin Newsom issued a shelter-in-place order for his state. He told people they must stay at home whenever possible. It was the first order of its kind in the United States, but other states soon followed.

THE NEW NORMAL

As shelter-in-place and stay-at-home orders spread across some parts of the nation, life changed in dramatic ways. Many businesses, schools, and churches closed their doors, and thousands of workers began to lose their jobs. Unemployment numbers soared. The stock

Governor Gavin Newsom of California issued the first shelter-in-place order in the United States on March 19, 2020.

market plunged. Uncertain of the future, people flocked to grocery stores to stock up on food and supplies. News footage showed people hoarding toilet paper, convinced there would soon be a shortage.

People struggled to adjust to stay-at-home orders. With schools closed, children began learning at home. Many parents needed to take time off from work to care for their kids. This was especially difficult for low-income and single-parent families. School districts and charities worked to feed children who relied on healthful school lunches. Workers who were able stayed at home to do

People waited in spread-out lines as stores and businesses began to enforce distancing rules.

their jobs remotely. Meanwhile, essential workers such as doctors, nurses, grocery store workers, and emergency responders continued to do their jobs in person despite the new risks.

Airline travel within the United States wasn't restricted. But thousands canceled travel plans, forcing airlines to cut thousands of flights. Despite the more frequent, serious warnings, some still went about life as normal. In Florida young adults on spring break flocked to crowded beaches.

The majority of people did pay attention to the viral threat. Normally crowded highways were deserted. Buses and commuter trains ran nearly empty. Because so few people were traveling, oil and gasoline prices plunged. As an unforeseen benefit, air pollution also dropped, improving global air quality.

A new normal began to emerge. Neighbors greeted one another from a distance. Handshakes and hugs were replaced by waves and nods. Families, friends, and coworkers met virtually instead of in person. Online video conference services such as Zoom and Skype helped to keep people connected. All around the country and the world, people found ways to connect at a distance.

The new normal came with a lot of difficulties. While many adjusted to social isolation and physical distancing,

The normally bustling Berlin-Tegel airport in Germany stood empty on May 20, 2020.

Around the world, many took to sticking hearts and other signs in their windows to thank healthcare and essential workers.

some suffered from depression and loneliness. Experts warned that long-term isolation could have negative effects on people's mental and physical health.

THE CRISIS DEEPENS

By April the United States had more COVID-19 cases than any other nation. All fifty states were affected. But New York—especially crowded New York City—was the hardest hit.

With millions in close contact, the virus could jump easily from host to host. In the first week of April, the state—driven by the crisis in the city—had more than five hundred deaths per day. One doctor described the scene in her hospital as apocalyptic. So many people were dying that there was nowhere to keep the bodies. Refrigerated trucks parked outside of hospitals to help hold the dead.

Inside the hospitals, doctors and nurses worked through challenging conditions. Shortages of gloves, masks, and other PPE increased the already high risk of exposure. They didn't have enough ventilators, medicine, or even beds for their patients.

On the Front Lines

In late March and early April, New York City was the center of the pandemic in the US. Twenty-seven-year-old Ashley Bray was one of the doctors on the front lines. Her 545-bed hospital was filled with COVID-19 patients, and many were in bad shape.

Despite a shortage of PPE, Bray went from patient to patient, caring for them as best she could. For many, she could do nothing. On one day, three of her patients died.

Because of the danger of infection, patients' families could not be with them. So Bray tried to help. She called patients' families so they could talk to their loved ones in their final moments. Bray and countless other doctors put in long hours in dangerous conditions to save lives.

Patients with the most severe cases had to fight for their lives. Many suffered pneumonia that left them unable to breathe. Their hearts worked harder and harder to pump blood and oxygen through their systems. For some patients, stress on their hearts led to cardiac arrest, or heart attacks.

"I'm seeing people who look relatively healthy . . . and they are completely wiped out, like they've been hit by a truck," said one respiratory therapist from Louisiana.

Those who caught COVID-19 described the experience to reporters. "Everything hurt," said a patient in Michigan. "I had a fever and chills. One minute my teeth

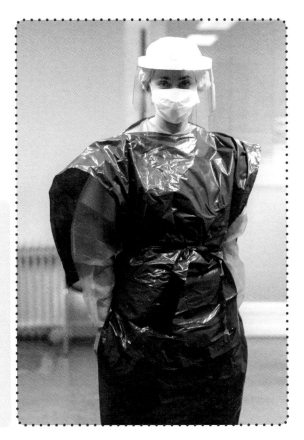

PPE shortages meant that many healthcare workers were forced to improvise protection, wearing items such as garbage bags and ski goggles.

Top 10 Hotspots in the United States

CANADA

Massachusetts

Illinois

New York

California

Pennsylvania

New Jersey

Arizona

N

Georgia

Texas

ATLANTIC
OCEAN

PACIFIC
OCEAN

MEXICO

Gulf of Mexico

Florida

Map date: 7/16/2020

Source: Johns Hopkins/CDC/USAToday

By mid-July, the US was dealing with its biggest outbreaks in these ten states.

are chattering and the next minute I am sweating like I am in a sauna. And the heavy, hoarse cough . . . rattled through my whole body."

As New York was fighting the outbreak, new hot spots emerged. Among them were New Orleans, Louisiana; Detroit, Michigan; and Chicago, Illinois. The outbreaks tended to hit densely populated urban areas the hardest. Due to systemic inequalities, Black and Brown people in these areas suffered a much higher rate of infection.

Stories about doctors, nurses, and patients fighting COVID-19 dominated news broadcasts. Experts feared that infections would spike over a short period in other areas the way they had in New York. States extended their orders to keep people apart. The goal was to flatten the curve, or ensure that infections were spread out over time so hospitals could handle them. Meanwhile, researchers worked to find effective treatments and improve testing for the virus, ultimately hoping to develop a vaccine.

Even as the crisis deepened, some people grew restless. In Michigan, Minnesota, and other states, groups protested stay-at-home orders. Protesters argued that state governments were overstepping their authority by

On April 15 armed protesters gathered at Michigan's State Capitol to voice their opposition to stay-at-home orders.

FAMILIES FIRST

From left: House Minority Leader Kevin McCarthy, House Speaker Nancy Pelosi, and House Majority Leader Steny Hoyer after the House passed the CARES Act on March 27

imposing widespread, long-term lockdowns. On April 17, Trump expressed support for these protesters on Twitter, implying that they were fighting for their freedom. The tweets alarmed public health experts, who warned against states loosening restrictions too soon. And a majority of Americans supported the protective measures.

As the lockdowns continued for months, the economy suffered. Some owners of small businesses begged to be allowed to open. They argued that their businesses could not survive much longer. Unemployed and underemployed people struggled to pay their bills. The federal government tried to help ease the financial stress of the lockdowns. In March Congress passed the CARES Act, which provided emergency funds to businesses

Feeding the Hungry

Michigan high school student Autumn Fitchett was ready for her senior prom. She'd been saving her money for the big event. But then came COVID-19. Her school was closed, and prom was canceled.

Fitchett understood that others were facing much bigger problems because of the pandemic. She watched as people lost their jobs and struggled to feed their families. Then she had an idea. She used the money she'd saved to buy food. She cleaned it, packed it in bags, and put it on a table outside her home. The food was free to anyone who needed it.

Fitchett's generous act gained a lot of attention, and her food pantry grew. She went from preparing a few dozen bags to preparing hundreds. She delivered many of them to older adults who were at the greatest risk from COVID-19.

and individuals. But even the funds that lasted longest expired by the end of July, and the government stalled on providing more help.

Those who believed the virus was not a threat argued more forcefully for states to reopen. Many more people were simply strained for income. They felt pressed into returning to work, even if they believed it was unsafe.

REOPENING AND CALLS FOR JUSTICE

By late April and early May, it was clear that physical distancing and stay-at-home orders were working. The spread of COVID-19 had slowed, and the overwhelming peak of cases that many experts feared had been largely avoided in most areas. As another bonus, physical distancing had also helped to slow the spread of other dangerous diseases such as the flu.

Many leaders believed it was time to start reopening the country. State governments took charge of their own reopening plans. They worked to provide guidelines that allowed their residents more freedom. The new restrictions varied from state to state. But all around the country,

A sign informs customers of COVID-19 restrictions at a store.

people started venturing out more and more. Restaurants that had been closed for months welcomed customers again. Beaches, playgrounds, and gyms followed. Many businesses had to take extra precautions such as allowing fewer customers and requiring everyone to wear masks.

Experts watched nervously. They knew that reopening the country would increase the spread of the disease. How much would depend on whether people would continue to follow health and safety guidelines. Would people still be careful to keep their distance? Would they wear masks while in public?

Meanwhile, an act of brutality changed everything. On May 25, police in Minneapolis, Minnesota, responded to a complaint at a local store. Four officers arrested a suspect, forty-six-year-old George Floyd. Officers claimed that Floyd, a Black man, resisted arrest. But video taken by a bystander showed a white officer, Derek Chauvin, pinning Floyd to the ground and placing a knee on his neck. A crowd begged Chauvin to stop. Despite the crowd and Floyd's cries for help, Chauvin pinned him for almost nine minutes, killing him.

The graphic and disturbing video made instant headlines. It recalled a long history of police brutality toward Black people and threw a spotlight on a deep rage and distrust in the Black community toward law enforcement. The next day, thousands took to the streets of Minneapolis to protest. Over the following week, the protests grew larger and spread around the nation and the world. People young and old, of all races, felt the

Above: Some protesters pointed out that COVID-19 had hit communities of color especially hard. *Below*: Community members in Minneapolis honored George Floyd with a painted mural.

Helping and Healing

Kelly Sherman-Conroy, a Native theologian and activist in Minneapolis, felt the hurt of her community after George Floyd's killing. So she sent out a call to action. She invited local religious and mental health leaders to serve wherever they were needed.

Over one hundred helpers responded. Wearing masks labeled Chaplain, they passed out water at protests and volunteered at food distribution sites. Often they led a prayer or listened to someone who needed to talk. "We do whatever we're asked to do," Sherman-Conroy said.

need to gather and speak out against racism and police brutality. Knowing the dangers posed by COVID-19, most protesters wore masks. They believed gathering was worth the risk. "We have been social distancing to the max—working from home, staying inside, quarantining—all of the above," said one protester. "This is our first time out in actual public, and it's for this, and I think that says something."

Later, the fears of many experts came true. As the country reopened, new cases surged in places that had initially avoided large outbreaks. Texas, Florida, and Arizona were among the states hit hardest. Through July and August, the United States topped four million and then five million confirmed cases, by far the most in

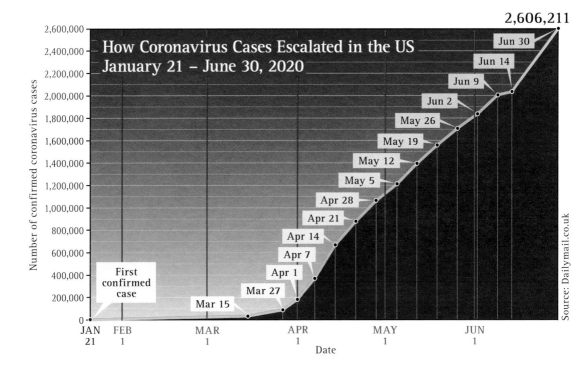

How Coronavirus Cases Escalated in the US
January 21 – June 30, 2020

Number of confirmed coronavirus cases

2,606,211

Jun 30
Jun 14
Jun 9
Jun 2
May 26
May 19
May 12
May 5
Apr 28
Apr 21
Apr 14
Apr 7
Apr 1
Mar 27
Mar 15

First confirmed case

Date

JAN 21 | FEB 1 | MAR 1 | APR 1 | MAY 1 | JUN 1

Source: Dailymail.co.uk

the world. The number continued to grow rapidly. Many states were forced to roll back their reopening plans. In October Trump contracted the virus and was hospitalized for several days before recovering.

SEARCHING FOR SOLUTIONS

Since COVID-19 is a global threat, government officials, public health experts, and scientists have strategized the best ways to fight it. The first line of defense is prevention. As states reopened in June, many recommended or required that citizens wear masks and stay six feet (2 m) apart from those outside their households. Cloth or paper masks do not filter out every piece of virus from the air. But they do lower the risk of spread, especially when worn by infected people. Other forms of prevention, such as hand-washing and physical distancing, also help to limit viral exposure.

The next line of defense is knowing who has the virus and with whom the infected have been in contact. Some countries traced infections more successfully than others. South Korea, for example, responded quickly to early outbreaks. The country tested widely and helped to limit the virus's spread by tracking and quarantining infected people.

Other nations, including the United States, lagged behind. Shortages of materials to make and perform tests, such as laboratory equipment and certain chemicals, limited states' testing capacity. Often only people who were already showing symptoms were even eligible to be tested. So those who carried the virus but didn't show symptoms could go unnoticed and potentially continue to spread it. Even where testing was available, results sometimes did not come in for weeks, rendering the tests worthless.

Dr. Anthony Fauci, head of the National Institute of Allergy and Infectious Diseases, helped to lead the US response to the pandemic. In June he voiced concerns about the country's testing missing infected people who didn't show symptoms. "We now know the level of virus in an asymptomatic person is about the same as the level of virus in somebody who has symptoms," he said. "So it's like, oh my goodness, how do you address that?"

Dr. Anthony Fauci

As the COVID-19 pandemic took hold in the US, Dr. Anthony Fauci became the face of the federal government's response. Having spent over fifty years working in public health, he was the nation's top infectious disease expert. He had helped to manage many viral outbreaks including HIV, swine flu, and Ebola.

Fauci met often with Trump, spoke at some White House briefings, and testified to Congress about the state of the pandemic in the country. While some government officials preferred to downplay the threat the virus posed, Fauci became known for speaking about the pandemic straightforwardly. Throughout the pandemic, he emphasized the importance of physical distancing, testing, and mask wearing to stop the spread of disease.

People wait to be tested for COVID-19 at a site in New York City.

The next line of defense against COVID-19 is treatment. Early on, doctors felt helpless to stop the disease. Nothing they did seemed to matter. Even ventilators didn't appear to do a lot of good. Patients died despite the best technology and medical attention.

As the virus spread around the world, more and more resources went to finding treatments. Researchers saw mixed results with existing drugs such as the antiviral drug remdesivir. And tests showed that the steroid dexamethasone lowered death rates and helped some patients to recover more quickly. Researchers were also encouraged by the use of blood plasma donated by people who had recovered from COVID-19. Their immune systems produced antibodies to the virus which, when transferred to a new patient, could block it from attaching to and infecting more cells.

Treatments were a part of fighting off the disease. But the ultimate solution to the COVID-19 pandemic could be a vaccine, a drug that can prevent people from ever getting the disease. But no vaccine would be quickly available. Developing one might take a long time, and its success could not be guaranteed. After all, several types of coronavirus cause the common cold, and scientists

Vaccines have nearly erased diseases such as smallpox.

Surviving Two Pandemics

Sophie Avouris was a baby in Greece when the Spanish flu pandemic swept through Europe in 1918. She survived it. Then, 102 years later, she was part of another worldwide outbreak. Avouris came down with COVID-19 in March 2020.

She was more tired than usual and developed a fever. COVID-19 hits older adults especially hard. So when the 102-year-old became sick, her prospects looked grim.

But Avouris fought off the virus. She recovered, showing that COVID-19 was not always fatal for the very old. And she became one of the very few people in the world who could say she survived two global pandemics.

have yet to create an effective vaccine against it.

Because COVID-19 was much more dangerous than the common cold, the world's medical research resources turned toward finding a solution. By June 10, 2020, at least 160 possible vaccines were being studied. Among the most promising was the mRNA-1273 vaccine. The vaccine contained a genetic sequence that trained human cells to produce certain proteins. Once produced, the proteins triggered the right immune response to fight the virus. Other vaccines took different approaches. With massive funding, researchers could explore a wide range of possible solutions. Some hoped a vaccine could be ready by the end of 2020. Others believed that it would take much longer and that people might have to endure wave after wave of COVID-19 outbreaks before relief would come.

Many of the world's brightest scientific minds have worked hard to find a cure. But the future remains uncertain. Some wonder if the disease might be just the beginning. As humans continue to encroach on wild habitats, the risk that more viruses could jump from animals to humans grows. During the first two decades of the twenty-first century, a range of new viral outbreaks, from SARS and MERS to swine flu, appeared. Experts have long warned about the possibility of a devastating global pandemic. Lessons learned from the COVID-19 pandemic may help to prepare the world to fight the next one.

IMPORTANT DATES

December 1, 2019	The earliest symptoms suspected to be COVID-19 are reported in Wuhan, China.
December 30, 2019	Chinese ophthalmologist Li Wenliang posts a warning online to fellow doctors, describing a SARS-like infection spreading in Wuhan.
January 11, 2020	China reports the first known death from COVID-19, a sixty-one-year-old man from Wuhan.
January 21, 2020	The United States reports its first known COVID-19 case in Washington State.
February 29, 2020	The United States reports its first known death from COVID-19. Later, two deaths on February 26 were suspected to be due to the disease.
March 11, 2020	The NBA suspends its season after a player tests positive for COVID-19. Trump bans foreign nationals traveling from most European countries.

March 19, 2020	California governor Gavin Newsom issues a shelter-in-place order for his state, the first in the US. Many other states soon follow.
March 26, 2020	The United States reports more COVID-19 cases than any other country, becoming the new center of the global pandemic.
April 17, 2020	In a series of tweets, Trump encourages people to protest lockdown orders. Many states begin to reopen a few weeks later.
May 21, 2020	The total number of worldwide reported COVID-19 cases tops five million.
July 7, 2020	The United States reports a total of more than three million cases.
August 9, 2020	Reported cases in the US hit five million.

SOURCE NOTES

8 Thomas Lake, "He Was on a Ventilator, Fighting for His Life. A Stranger Sent Reinforcements," CNN, April 23, 2020, https://www.cnn.com/2020/04/22/opinions/coronavirus-plasma-donor/index.html.

16 Doug Bock Clark, "Inside the Nightmare Voyage of the *Diamond Princess*," *GQ*, April 30, 2020, https://www.gq.com/story/inside-diamond-princess-cruise-ship-nightmare-voyage.

18 David Knowles, "Trump Says Coronavirus Will 'Go Away without a Vaccine,' " Yahoo News, May 8, 2020, https://news.yahoo.com/trump-says-coronavirus-will-go-away-without-a-vaccine-195154249.html.

26 Lizzie Presser, "A Medical Worker Describes Terrifying Lung Failure from COVID-19—Even in His Young Patients," ProPublica.org, March 21, 2020, https://www.propublica.org/article/a-medical-worker-describes--terrifying-lung-failure-from-covid19-even-in-his-young-patients.

26–27 "'An Anvil Sitting on My Chest': What It's Like to Have Covid-19," *New York Times*, May 7, 2020, https://www.nytimes.com/article/coronavirus-symptoms.html?action=click&module=RelatedLinks&pgtype=Article.

34 Jean Hopfensperger, "Minnesota 'Crisis Mode Chaplains' Seek to Heal Trauma of George Floyd's Death," *Minneapolis Star Tribune*, July 6, 2020, https://www.startribune.com/crisis-mode-chaplains-seek-to-heal-trauma-of-floyd-s-death/571647852/?refresh=true.

34 Maggie Foxx, "Demonstrators Say It's Worth Braving
    Coronavirus to Protest George Floyd's Killing," CNN.com,
    June 6, 2020, https://www.cnn.com/2020/06/06/health/pandemic
    -protesters-covid-risk-floyd-trnd/index.html.

36 Jim Acosta and Sam Fossum, "Fauci Says Task Force 'Seriously
    Considering' New Testing Strategy," CNN, June 26, 2020,
    https://www.cnn.com/2020/06/26/politics/anthony-fauci-testing
    -coronavirus-task-force/index.html.

SELECTED BIBLIOGRAPHY

"Coronavirus." Centers for Disease Control and Prevention. Accessed August 8, 2020. https://www.cdc.gov/coronavirus/2019-ncov/index.html.

"Coronavirus (COVID-19)." National Institutes of Health. Last modified June 20, 2020. https://www.nih.gov/coronavirus.

"Coronavirus in the US: Latest Map and Case Count." *New York Times*, July 24, 2020. https://www.nytimes.com/interactive/2020 /us/coronavirus-us-cases.html?action=click&module=Top%20 Stories&pgtype=Homepage.

"Global Research on Coronavirus Disease (COVID-19)." World Health Organization. Accessed July 24, 2020. https://www.who.int /emergencies/diseases/novel-coronavirus-2019/global-research -on-novel-coronavirus-2019-ncov.

Johns Hopkins University & Medicine: Coronavirus Resource Center. Accessed August 18, 2020. https://coronavirus.jhu.edu/.

"The latest on the coronavirus pandemic." CNN.com, August 18, 2020. https://www.cnn.com/world/live-news/coronavirus-pandemic-08-18 -20-intl/index.html.

"A Timeline of the Coronavirus Pandemic." *New York Times*, August 6, 2020. https://www.nytimes.com/article/coronavirus-timeline.html.

LEARN MORE

BrainPOP: Coronavirus
https://www.brainpop.com/health/diseasesinjuriesandconditions
/coronavirus/

Levine, Sara. *Germs Up Close.* Minneapolis: Millbrook Press, 2021.

London, Martha. *The Spread of COVID-19.* Minneapolis: Core Library, 2021.

National Geographic Kids: Facts about Coronavirus
https://kids.nationalgeographic.com/science/article/facts-about-coronavirus

INDEX